Splish Splash Splosh!

by Mick Manning
and
Brita Granström

W
FRANKLIN WATTS
A Division of Grolier Publishing
NEW YORK • LONDON • HONG KONG • SYDNEY
DANBURY, CONNECTICUT

Splish, Splash, Splosh!

Waves hit the beach.
They come roaring in only to trickle away.
Where do they come from and where do they go?

Waves are caused by the winds and tides.

Splish, Splash, Splosh!

Waves dance near the shore –
slop under boats and ships,
slap against harbors and jetties.

A   ferry

A   tugboat

A   tanker

Splish, Splash, Splosh!

Far out to sea where the water is deep, seawater washes over dolphins' backs and between sharks' teeth...slips through shipwrecks and coral reefs.

Parts of the sea are so deep huge mountain ranges can lie under the surface.

Giant octopuses and many other creatures live deep under the sea.

Splish, Splash, Splosh!

On hot days, the sun sucks tiny droplets of water into the sky. Clouds form and drift above the crashing waves. Sea breezes blow them far away – high in the sky they sail inland like ships.

Clouds are formed from tiny droplets of water.

Sometimes frogs and even small fish can be sucked up into the clouds and fall with the rain somewhere else!

Splish, Splash, Splosh!

Clouds heavy with water gather over the land and swirl into a storm. Raindrops burst from the clouds and fall to earth.

Some countries have rainstorms called monsoons. Monsoons can destroy buildings and flood towns.

Different sorts of clouds...

fine day clouds

thunder clouds

grey day clouds

11

Splish, Splash, Splosh!

Rainwater trickles down the hillsides...
makes puddles...flows wild and muddy
into streams.

Every living thing needs water to survive!

Splish, Splash, Splosh!

Streams rush headlong into a crazy waterfall,
that crashes into a river that swells and swells...
and fills up a dam.

A rainbow is made when the sun shines through tiny drops of water in the air.

The colors of a rainbow are red, orange, yellow, green, blue, indigo, and violet...

Splish, Splash, Splosh!

In the dam, muddy water clears.
Fish live in the dam; they swim around a pipe
that takes the water down to filters and
cleaning tanks.

Water must be cleaned before we can drink it ...

Dams, reservoirs, and underground wells are places where we store water.

In times of drought when there is not much rain, water has to be delivered by tanker.

Splish, Splash, Splosh!

Water travels for miles – under fields, hills, roads, and motorways to an underground reservoir. Then it joins the main water supply to towns, villages, factories, hotels, offices, and houses... to your house!

Water has many uses, we can drink it, wash with it, heat it to keep our houses warm, water plants with it, and flush toilets with it...

underground reservoir- stores the water

↑screening tanks↑ removes large pieces of dirt

filter bed ↗ takes away all dirt.

Chlorine is added here to kill all germs.

water mai

18

← S-trap

An S-trap keeps stale water from coming back up the pipe and keeps away nasty smells and germs.

Splish, Splash, Splosh!

You take a shower.
Clean water splutters out of the taps...
out of the showerhead. Then soapy
water escapes down the the drain.

Rats are very common down sewers all over the world. They spread diseases so some cities employ "ratcatchers".

Splish, Splash, Splosh!

Under the street, bathwater mixes with other waste water – sink water and toilet water.

Sometimes unwanted pets - tropical fish and even alligators have been found in sewers. They'd been flushed down the toilet!

It runs along sewer tunnels as big as subways and becomes thick and sludgy.

Splish, Splash, Splosh!

Waste water flows out into the waste disposal site.
It pushes through sieves, dribbles through screens,
squeezes through filters, and bubbles through blowers.
Water leaves sludge behind and is piped out.
It trickles and gushes back to the...

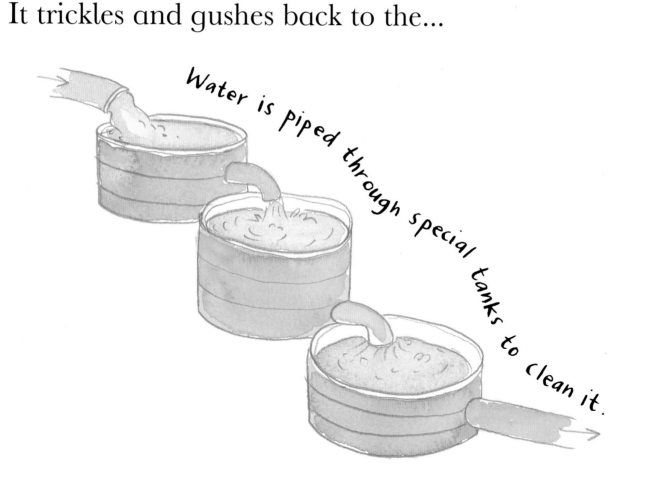

Water is piped through special tanks to clean it.

Sea!

Splish, Splash, Splosh!

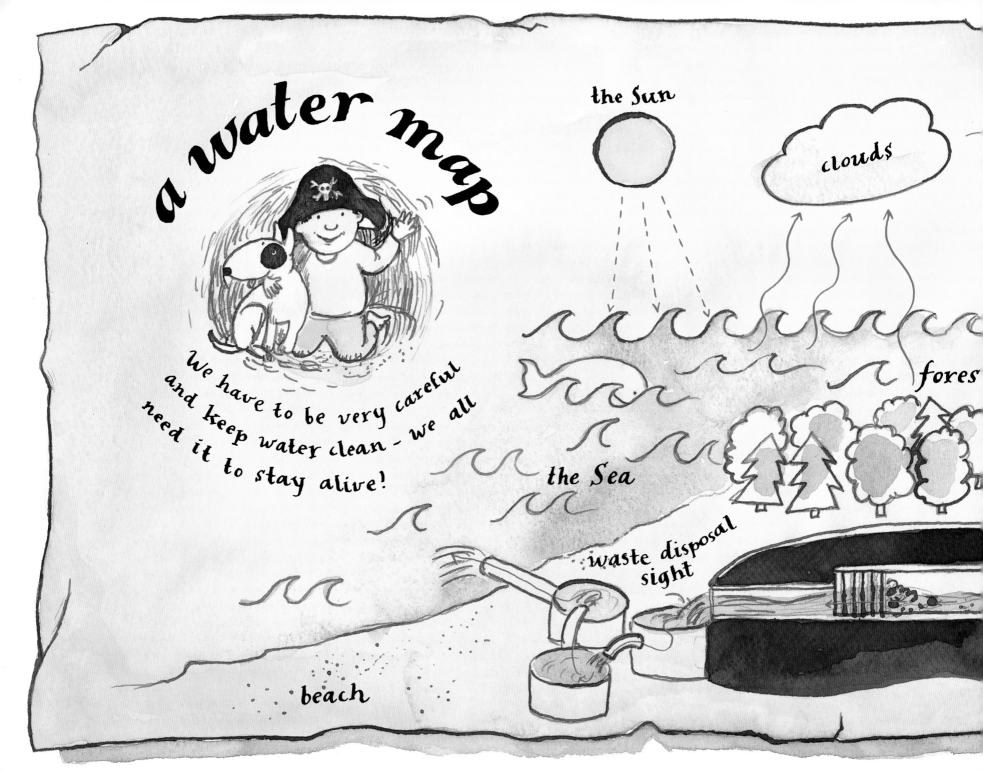

a water map

We have to be very careful and keep water clean – we all need it to stay alive!

the Sun

clouds

the Sea

fores

waste disposal
sight

beach

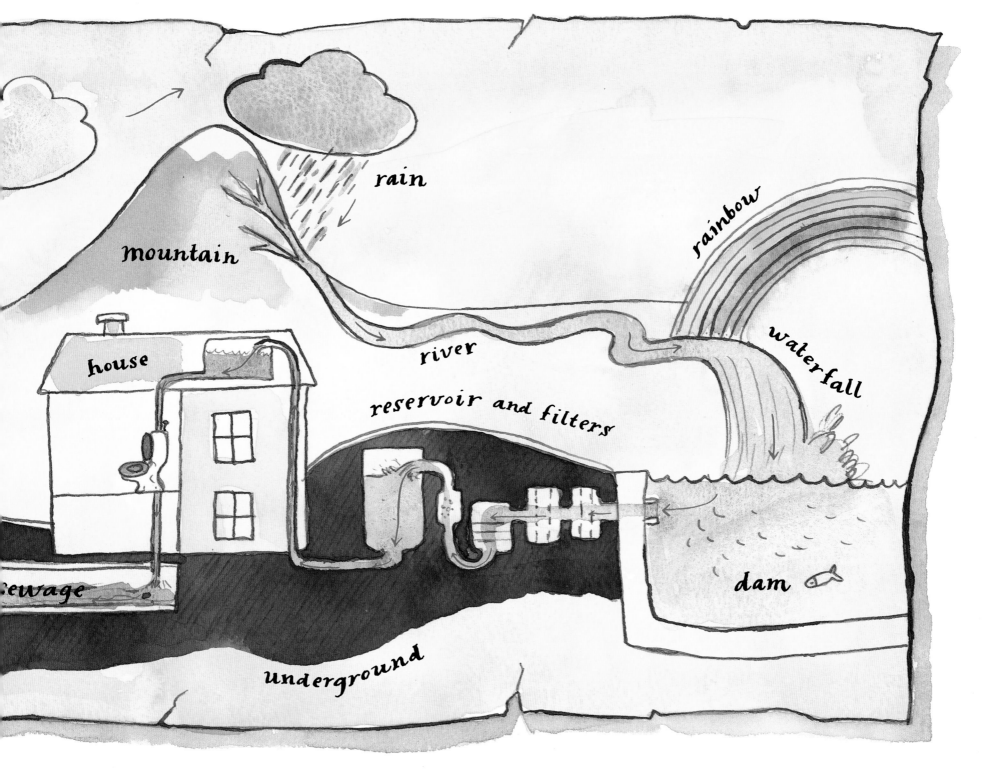

rain

mountain

rainbow

waterfall

house

river

reservoir and filters

sewage

dam

underground

Helpful words

Alligators are big animals like crocodiles (see page 23). They live in the United States of America or China.

Chlorine is a substance that is put into water to kill germs (see page 18).

Clouds are huge white or grey shapes made from millions of small drops of water (see pages 9-11).

Coral reefs are made up of tiny sea animals that grow rocky shells and live together in warm seas (see page 7).

Dams and reservoirs are places where water is stored (see pages 14-17).

Evaporation is the way tiny drops of water are sucked into the air on warm days (see page 8). Tiny drops of water are also sucked out of plant leaves into the air on warm days (see page 28).

Ferries carry passengers and cars across stretches of water (see page 4).

Filter is a type of screen which keeps dirt back and lets clean water through (see page 18, 25, 28)

Harbors and jetties are special sheltered places where boats are kept (see page 4).

Monsoons are rainstorms that last for months in some hot countries (see page 11).

Sewage is the dirty water from toilets and drains (see pages 22-25).

Shipwreck is a sunken ship (see page 7).

Tugboats are used to tow other boats (see page 4).

Tanker ships carry oil and petrol across the sea (see page 4).

Tanker trucks carry liquids from place to place by road (see page 17).

S-trap is a pipe under the sink or a bath that keeps germs and smells from coming up (see page 20).

Waste disposal site is where sewage water is cleaned (see pages 24-25).

Water power the power of moving water can be used to turn a wheel or work a machine to make electricity (see pages 14-15).

© 1997 Franklin Watts
First American Edition 1997 by
Franklin Watts, A division of Grolier Publishing
90 Sherman Turnpike, Danbury, CT 06816
Text and illustrations © 1997 Mick Manning
and Brita Granström
Series editor: Paula Borton
Art director: Robert Walster
Consultant: Peter Riley
Printed in Singapore

Library of Congress Cataloging-in-Publication Data
Manning, Mick
    Splish,Splash, Splosh! : a book about water / by Mick Manning and
    Brita Granström -- 1st American ed.
        p. cm. -- (Wonderwise)
    Summary : Illustrations and simple text discuss water, where it comes from and
how it is treated so that we can use it for drinking, washing, and playing.
        ISBN 0-531-14488-7 (hb). -- ISBN 0-531-15326-6 (pbk.)
        1. Water--Juvenile literature. [1. Water.] I. Granström, Brita.
        II. Title. III. Series.
        GB662.3M36   1997
    553.7--DC21   97-16325
                                                                    CIP
                                                                    AC